EARTH HEROES! HELP SAVE OUR PLANET

Conservation for Kids

Children's Conservation Books

All Rights reserved. No part of this book may be reproduced or used in any way or form or by any means whether electronic or mechanical, this means that you cannot record or photocopy any material ideas or tips that are provided in this book.

Copyright 2016

HOW MUCH DO YOU LOVE OUR HOME PLANET—THE EARTH?

Problems like global warming, endangered animals, flooding, and pollution in the oceans pose a dreadful threat to Earth and its life forms.

WHAT COULD BE DONE TO SAVE EARTH?

Let's join hands to make a difference!

Kids, you can do it with your own little ways. Earth heroes be like...

CONSERVE WATER

Help conserve water. Begin at home. Take measures to not use more water than you need. Don't waste it.

Water shortages have an impact to our planet. Fix leaky faucets. Water-saving devices have to be installed on your faucets.

Don't run the dish washer until it is full. While brushing your teeth, don't leave the faucet running.

USE FEWER CHEMICALS

Cut back on the use of chemicals you use in your homes and cars.

These chemicals are harmful to the water supply and to your health. These can be carried to waterways and aquatic life without us knowing it.

DISPOSE TOXIC WASTE PROPERLY

Harmful chemicals should not be put into sewers, rivers, lakes or any body of water.

Learn about best practices for disposing of these harmful wastes before it's too late.

IDENTIFY AND REPORT LARGE-SCALE POLLUTERS

We should help to keep our water sources clean.

Industries and factories are often found to cause both air and water pollution. Speak up and protect the earth.

You may also volunteer and join environmental groups to clean up the surroundings. Invite your friends to join. Be active and be involved.

PRESERVE AIR QUALITY BY REDUCING AIR POLLUTION.

You can do this by using less electricity.

Burning coal and natural gas to make electricity is a major factor in air pollution. Your reliance on electricity must be reduced.

Solar power is a great option for use at home, especially for heating water. When you leave home, electrical equipment should be shut off.

TURN OFF APPLIANCES WHEN NOT IN USE.

The most basic, yet the most effective, thing to do is to plant more trees.

Deforestation should be discouraged. Reforestation should be encouraged.

EAT LOCALLY-GROWN FOODS

Industrial farming is unsafe for our planet. It is harmful. When you buy food, don't forget to check where it comes from.

Eat more locally-grown vegetables and fruits rather than foods that have to come long distances to you.

This world is ours. Earth is the only planet that can sustain life. Would you want it to be destroyed?

All living creatures that we know of live here. Among the living creatures, humans are considered as the most intelligent.

So we can think of the best things to do to save the Earth and all its inhabitants.

It is indeed our responsibility to restore and preserve our green Earth.

IT'S A PRIVILEGE TO HELP!
WHY NOT BEGIN TODAY?

www.ingramcontent.com/pod-product-compliance
Lightning Source LLC
LaVergne TN
LVHW061322060426
835507LV00019B/2261